Dyar
AF544743

Faces of Texas

By
Gilbert J. Jordan

EAKIN PRESS
Austin, Texas

Published in the United States of America
By Eakin Press, P.O. Box 23066
Austin, Texas 78735

ISBN 0-89015-403-1

Dedicated to the people of Texas with their colorful history and lore, to the pioneers and their struggles, to the various ethnic groups and their heritage, and to all who helped shape the Lone Star State.

(Close-up view of wooden windmill, Old City Park, Dallas. Photo by Cary Ferguson, 1981).

PREFACE

The present book deals with some of the natural phenomena and beauties of the state of Texas, its colorful history, its people, their ethnic background, folklore, cultural heritage, and customs. The subject matter and the themes of the poems were chosen because of their importance and relevance to life in Texas, both past and present. The scope and nature of the work permitted only sketchy vignettes, rather than broad and complete pictures of the state and its people. Only a few characteristic features or personality traits were selected and presented in each case.

The poems appear in traditional style and rhymed lines. They are easily accessible because they are intentionally slanted to appeal to perceptive general readers. However, in spite of my efforts to compose understandable verse, I did use some less familiar words, allusions, and foreign expressions that are inherent in the subject matter, but may not readily be clear without explanation. For this reason, I prepared an index of words and names and included it in the back of the book. All items in the index are arranged alphabetically and explained, translated, or identified as needed.

Some of the poems were written earlier and published in my volume of verse entitled *The Morning Is Not Far*, Dallas, 1974, but most of them were composed recently at the suggestion of Edwin M. Eakin in anticipation of the approaching sesquicentennial of Texas independence (1836-1986). It is my hope that the poems will lead to further reading and study of the rich lore of Texas and the Texans. For this reason a Bibliography of suggested readings is included. These books served as sources of information and confirmation.

Most of the pictures are photographic prints of people and scenes, and some are reproductions of sketches and paintings. In all cases proper acknowledgements are given along with the illustrations. To the people who provided me with photographs or assisted in the collecting of the pictures I am indeed grateful.

I am especially indebted to Lora B. Bowyer, my son Dr. Terry G. Jordan, my wife Vera Tiller Jordan, and the late Margaret Blum for reading the manuscript carefully and making suggestions for improvement and for additional poems.

Gilbert J. Jordan
Dallas, Texas, 1983

CONTENTS

Faces of Texas

IMMIGRANTS ALL

Anglos came to this land they loved,
And Poles to Panna Maria moved;
From Germany and Mexico
They came to Texas their seed to sow.

They lived in a Coushatta haunt,
Dutch Nederland and in Beaumont.
Chalk Mountain folk raised Indian corn
And stored it in a Swiss-style barn.

The Amerinds made woodland trails,
And Chinese helped to build the rails.
Italians found their little niche,
And Scandanavians had their wish.

The Irish came from an isle of green
And built their homes on the Texas scene.
All came together; their heritage blends:
Cajuns, Blacks, and Czechs, and Wends.

Who are these people who filled up the land?
Defended it and took their stand?
They are the Texans, immigrants all;
They saw the star and heard its call.

"Anglos came to this land they loved."
("Pioneer," painting by William Tylee Ramey, 1813-1856. Photo, Eugene C. Barker Texas History Center, The University of Texas.)

AN EARLY IMMIGRANT SEES TEXAS, 1845

No fir tree grows on Texas soil,
Nor blooms the linden tree;
Here grow mesquite and cedar woods;
The sun bears down on me.

The Indians hunt the buffalo
On prairies and on plains,
While in the grass hiss rattlesnakes
Harsh melodies and pains.

How vast this varied countryside,
Still waiting for a change!
The peasants will be cowboys here
And ride across the range.

"While in the grass hiss rattlesnakes
Harsh melodies and pains."
(Photo, in the Austin-Travis County Collection, Austin Public Library.)

THE PIONEER AT INDIANOLA

He first saw Texas when German settlers came
To build anew in eighteen forty-five.
By rocky mesas lay his deeded claim,
Still waiting for a new age to arrive.

But on the lonely Gulf of Mexico
The fever spread; his dearest loved one died;
At Indianola, menacing and low,
He buried her, and in his sorrow cried:

"The land is new and great, so we were told,
And hope and happiness await the brave;
But now my hopes of life are withered, old,
As in my grief I look upon her grave."

Now love lies buried in the salty sands,
His heart is heavy as though filled with stones;
His head is bowed, and helpless are his hands,
The mist reverberates with troubled moans.

Then where the ashy sea fowls soar and fly,
He sees the boats go silently away;
And angry, threat'ning winds come rushing by
To lash the saddened spirit by the bay.

And now his soul is like the flight of gulls
Far out upon the restless, rolling sea;
His body like the empty, broken hulls
Of battered skiffs blown over on the lee.

"He first saw Texas when German settlers came
To build anew in eighteen forty-five."

("Emigrants in Bremerhaven," painting by Johannes Gehrts, Photo, courtesy, the Focke-Museum, Bremen.)

TO AN ANCIENT OAK

1. Alcalde

You were a judge so dread
Upon the far-spread prairie,
You hanged men limp and dead
From strong and hairy
Arms. Your mossy face,
A pale and eerie place,
Betokens ghastly sights
Of lynchings in the nights.

2. Camp Meeting

Cathedral on the endless plains,
Groined like Gothic window panes —
Men sang hymns and prayed to God,
While kneeling on the spongy sod.

3. Patriarch

You are the patriarch, the seer,
The Moses of the plains.
You led the early pioneer
In covered-wagon trains
Across the far-spread land.
You saw him die without a fear.
You are the hand
That held command
Over a hemisphere.

"You led the early pioneer
In covered-wagon trains
Across the far-spread land."

(Large live oak tree with Spanish moss, near Goliad. Photo in the R. B. Pumphrey Collection, Eugene C. Barker Texas History Center, The University of Texas.)

SAN JOSÉ, GEM OF THE MISSIONS

In San Antone stands Mission San José,
An edifice that will to all display
The Indian times and Spanish *padre's* labors,
Their blessings, music, hardships, and their favors.

Saint Joseph's Church was like a mighty fortress.
A stronghold in a cruel wilderness.
The Spaniards brought security and order
To troubled men across the Texas border.

The church is set just like a precious stone
Into a ring of smaller huts. Alone
Its ornate and Baroque façade once faced
The desert land by which it was embraced.

Franciscan friars brought hispanic art
And built a church of God that stands apart.
It tells the world that this is still a shrine,
Where people's souls can see spirit shine.

"Saint Joseph's Church was like a mighty fortress,
A stronghold in a cruel wilderness."
(Photo by the author.)

TEXAS HAD NO PLYMOUTH ROCK

Texas had no Plymouth Rock,
But it had land, and land, and land.
To this the people would rush and flock;
A new migration would take command.

The Spaniards knew this, but didn't know
That empty land would call abroad,
And others would immigrate and grow
Their civilization on foreign sod.

The Mexicans did not realize
That men across the Rio Grande
Loved freedom as a precious prize;
And for their land would make a stand.

And thus it was; the people came;
They sowed their seed in Texas soil.
Some fought the battles and won their fame,
And all built houses by skill and toil.

"Texas had no Plymouth Rock,
But it had land, and land, and land."
(Scene on Padre Island. Photo by R. H. Veeder, Dallas, 1975.)

REMEMBER THE ALAMO

The soldiers stormed the Alamo,
And the battle was won by Mexico.
The defense of the Texans could not withstand
The hordes under Santa Anna's command;
Soon waves of Mexicans broke through.
What could the men in the Alamo do?
"They are upon us — now give 'em hell!"
Cried Travis, and his men fought well.
"Aim and fire; hold back the flood;
The enemy must pay in blood."
The "Devil Texans" the attack defied;
Like paladins they fought and died.
The Mexicans paid a price, too high;
They won and lost; the end was nigh.
The Texans had given their lives for a cause;
This wasn't the end; this was a pause.
The battle was lost, but the war was won;
The dawn of another day had begun.
The word of the bloody slaughter spread.
"Remember the Alamo," the Texans said;
"Remember Goliad, remember the dead."
And thus the scene for revenge was laid.
Sam Houston took up the battle cry.
He didn't stand around and sigh;
He attacked the enemy one day
And settled accounts in his own way.

"The battle was lost, but the war was won;
The dawn of another day had begun."

(Present-day view of the restored Alamo. Photo, in the Eugene C. Barker Texas History Center, The University of Texas.)

THE RAVEN

He left his state of Tennessee
And lived the life of a Cherokee.
He was the Indians' friend, and they
Adopted him and bade him stay.

He went away; to Texas he came;
And there he found a life of fame.
No chance to save the Alamo.
At San Jacinto he put on his show.

He beat old Santa Anna there
And freed the people from despair;
In *siesta* time for the Mexicans,
He won the war for the Texicans.

Then he repented and was saved;
They baptized him, and he behaved,
But the fish in the *Brazos de Dios* were stained
By sin and pollution, so he maintained.

His six foot six, more or less,
Was a mighty package of stubbornness.
He joined the state to the USA,
And opposed the ones who took it away.

He was a unionist at heart
And would not break the nation apart.
Sam Houston loved his country whole;
This was his mission; this, his goal.

"Sam Houston loved his country whole.
This was his mission; this, his goal."

(The Seymour Thomas portrait of Houston. Photo of the portrait, San Jacinto Museum of History Association.)

COTTON GROWS, 1860

Cotton grows in one man' field;
Another man hoes and picks the yield.
"Grab that sack and get to work;
Bend your back; no time to shirk."

Cotton was king; the plantation, big.
"No time to sing, nor dance a jig."
In the South was heard the rumbling of war;
Just mark my word, it's not too far.

The great plantations all slept too late,
Heard incantations of war and hate.
The people burned King Cotton down;
His destiny turned; he lost his crown.

The hapless poor soon fell and died;
Death was sure, and none could hide.
But cotton survived on western plains,
Where it revived to make new gains.

"Cotton grows in one man's field;
Another man hoes and picks the yield."

(Cotton Picking," painting by Oscar Berninghous. Photo of painting, courtesy, Eugene C. Barker Texas History Center, The University of Texas.)

THE FREDERICKSBURG COFFEEMILL

The building was a funny little fortress
That served as church, as school, and city hall.
At first all faiths assembled here like Pilgrims,
But no one ever could unite them all.

For half a century it calmly stood;
Half-timbered plastered walls were firm and strong.
The people gathered here in times of hunger
And prayed for food and for relief from wrong.

The troubled citizens held meetings here,
And here they oft discussed the common dangers,
How they might live in peace with Indians,
And how to guard against all hostile strangers.

The cupola above served well as lookout;
From here the people watched the spreading land.
These were the Indians' favorite hunting grounds,
And here might lurk a vigilante band.

It was rebuilt in nineteen thirty-five.
Its present face again to us recalls
The troubled times of early pioneers
Who raised the old, unique, eight-sided walls.

"The people gathered here in times of hunger
And prayed for food and for relief from wrong."

(The original Fredericksburg coffeemill, *Kaffeemühle*, community building and church, *Vereinskirche*, built in 1847, razed in 1897, and rebuilt in 1935.)

MEUSEBACH MOON

"We'll meet again when the moon is full,"
Said Comanche chief, big Katemoczy,
To red-beard Meusebach, *El Sol*,
"On Rio San Saba our camp will be."

And when the moon was full again,
They met beneath the open sky;
The white man and the Indian
Agreed on peace by the sun on high.

The peace pipe made the circle round,
While chiefs and settlers took an oath;
The Whites and Indians sat on the ground,
And the future promised peace for both.

To settlers' "wigwams" the red men came,
And gifts were paid for Indian lands;
Twice rounded was the moon, the same,
But hunting grounds slipped from their hands.

"The peace pipe made the circle round,
While chiefs and settlers took an oath."

(Imaginary scene of the Meusebach Indian peace treaty. After a painting by Mrs. Ernest Marschall, daughter of John O. Meusebach. Courtesy, Pioneer Museum, Fredericksburg.)

THE STAMPEDE

The buffaloes, the buffaloes,
Before the prairie fire they run;
They stir up dust that fills the sky
And dims and hides the evening sun.

Then driven by an inner fear,
They thunder on in a wild stampede;
No stopping them; the storm is here,
And those that fall are trampled and bleed.

Like a mighty tornado they rush along,
Cleft hooves are pounding and cutting the ground.
Where will they go? How will they stop?
When will it cease, this threat'ning sound?

The fire races, the wild beasts flee;
Destruction and dying everywhere.
The fire stretches its blazing tongue;
The animals' breath is steaming air.

The buffaloes yielded to longhorn cattle
And then experienced the Indians' fate.
No more stampedes; the storm subsided;
No place for bisons in the lone star state.

"The buffaloes, the buffaloes,
Before the prairie fire they run."

(Photo by N. H. Rose. R. B. Pumphrey Collection, Eugene C. Barker Texas History Center, The University of Texas.)

CHIEF QUANAH PARKER

He was the last; he came too late.
His mother was Cynthia Ann Parker, a White;
Peta Nocona took her for his mate;
Their son was Quanah, who fought with might.

Yes, Quanah Parker was a warrior chief,
He commanded Quahadi-Comanche braves;
As their leader in him they placed their belief;
They stood by him as though his slaves.

At Adobe Walls he saved his life
While fighting buffalo hunters there;
At Palo Duro he escaped the strife
To fight again for the Indian's share.

But he saw the sunset of Amerinds;
Their days were ended by MacKenzie's men.
Comanches were blown away by the winds,
And none was left to fight again.

Quanah rode the Texas trails,
But Oklahoma became his home;
No more Battles of Adobe Walls,
No buffalo hunting, no chance to roam.

The iron horse soon took the place
Of the pony on which he led his fight.
No hunting now, no battles, no chase;
And this was Quanah Parker's plight.

"No hunting now, no battles, no chase:
And this was Quanah Parker's plight."
(Photo, courtesy, Maxeen Bridwell, Five Civilized Tribes Museum, Muskogee, Oklahoma.)

PIONEER WOMAN

When the men are far away on roundups,
She keeps her rifle ready.
To guard her home and save her children
Her aim is sure and steady.

For many days and weeks she watches
In loneliness and fear;
She has to be the home's protector
When no one else is near.

The wild men come to steal and kill,
And she is all alone;
She bolts the doors and guards the children,
Afraid to cry or moan.

She hears so many sounds at night,
A bellowing bull or an owl.
The wilds around are full of sounds;
Coyotes begin to howl.

This time the Indians did not attack;
There's respite for the day.
Tonight the sounds will come again.
Would they might go away.

"When the men are far away on roundups,
She keeps her rifle ready."

(Photo from the Papers of Mr. and Mrs. Joseph E. Taulman, The Eugene C. Barker Texas History Center, The University of Texas at Austin.)

THE COWBOY'S GOODBYE

My saddle is rocking on the plain:
I'll never see my home again.
We are saying "Goodbye," my pony and I,
We are going away to our home in the sky.

And the heavens above, like a mighty tree,
Are spread o'er the West as far as I see;
With my feet in the stirrups, my eyes far away,
I am singing and riding all the day.

"We are saying 'Goodbye,' my pony and I,
We are going away to our home in the sky."

(A cowboy, *vaquero*, of the brush country. Photo, in the Eugene C. Barker Texas History Center, The University of Texas.)

THE ROUNDUP

Once when the land was open and wide,
Men hunted the prairies for buffalo hide.
Then cattle came to the hills and vales,
And cowboys in camps told rustic tales.

Did you ever hear of old man Cooter?
He rode a black horse and packed a six-shooter.
To his saddle were tied a rope and a whip;
Don't make him angry, or he'll end your trip.

Now rope the calves and put on his brand;
Don't ask any questions, or you'll bite the sand.
Next year you'll round them up to sell;
Don't talk too much, or you'll land in hell.

The drovers take the herds up north;
They sell them in Kansas for what they are worth.
If they get home with the money they made,
They'll buy more land, and cash must be paid.

The ranchmen stretched fences across the range;
No place to roam when they've made this change.
And Cooter said: "Don't fence me in,"
But he had to lose, so the ranchers could win.

"Now rope the calves and put on his brand;
Don't ask any questions, or you'll bite the sand."

(Photo by Erwin E. Smith, in the Texas Memorial Museum, The University of Texas at Austin.)

TO AN OLD ROCK FENCE

As rugged as the pioneer
Who built your sturdy forms,
You stand and hold what he has won;
you stretch out heavy arms.

He poured no mortar in your veins
And fashioned not a stone;
His heavy blood cemented you;
He shaped you with a groan.

You fell from him as burdens fall,
You grew as hope has grown;
And in your dusty face is seen
The struggle he has known.

Your mighty limbs are reaching out
Beyond his distant gaze
And gath'ring to his yearning heart
The vision of his days.

"His heavy blood cemented you;
He shaped you with a groan."
(Rock fence in Mason County. Photo by the author, 1977.)

BIG BEND COUNTRY

Blue mountains call you from afar to come:
"We'll keep you safe; we'll be your western home.
Before you, lie the valleys and river plains,
A spreading vista that in the distance wanes.
You can behold the shimmering air and space
That quake before the mighty mountain's face.
It is so far and near, so rough and fair.
Here you can meet the sun; its splendor share.
Who knows a better place to breathe the sky
And feel infinity than here on high?"

"Before you lie the valleys and river plains,
A spreading vista that in the distance wanes."

(Scene in the Big Bend National Park. Photo, in the Eugene C. Barker Texas History Center, The University of Texas.)

GREAT RIVER

I am the clouds, I am the falling sky,
The melting snow, the rain, the stream am I.

First, like a youth who's skiing down the hill,
I speed along, and on the falls I spill.

I reach the plains and saunter through the weeds,
I comb the grass and brush away the seeds.

I wash your fields and spread them out to dry;
Your towns I cleanse; your cities, purify.

And waters from the mountain cry to me:
"Oh Brother, take us with you to the sea."

All through the endless years I wander on,
And still I'm with you at each waking dawn.

Through timeless ages I have carved the ground;
Along the path my handiworks abound.

I saturate the earth, the thirsty sand;
And leave behind me cities, spreading land.

"I reach the plains and saunter through the weeds,
I comb the grass and brush away the seeds."
(Flooded stream in West Texas. Photo by the author, 1976.)

I am your bread, your water, and your light;
I come to bless or curse you with my might.

I also am the storm, the surging flood,
The pulpy drift, the silt, and clammy mud.

I soil your streets, I fill your house with waves,
Defile your beds, engulf ancestral graves.

I am a ship, I carry in my hold
Your fertile fields, your land, your shining gold.

These treasures then I take to Father Sea;
With opened arms he takes and welcomes me.

"I am a ship, I carry in my hold
Your fertile fields, your land, your shining gold."

(Santa Elena Canyon of the Rio Grande in the Big Bend National Park. From the R. B. Pumphrey Collection in the Eugene C. Barker Texas History Center, The University of Texas.)

WINDMILLS (SIX IMAGES)

1. Blue Norther

You are whirling the wind along
And singing a song,
While blowing the air
Like a fan in the sky.
And the heavens rush by,
Twisting your hair
In silvery strands.
Then you chase the wind and clouds
And swing your twirling hands
In flying shrouds
Of dusty air.

2. Weather Vane

You are a landmark in the sky
When you hold your head up high.
With a humming sound,
You are turning around
Like a weather vane
With a galvanized plane,
Showing the wind where to go,
When to stop, when to blow.

3. Prairie Schooner

With your flag on the mast
You are sailing along
Till your anchor is cast
Where the cool waters throng
In pulsating underground veins.
To the rocks below,
Where fresh waters flow,
You tell your tale
Of clouds and of gale
And of winds that blow o'er the plains.

"You are a landmark in the sky
When you hold your head up high."
(Windmill and "tank" in Dallas, Dallas County. Photo by the author, 1981.)

4. Vaquero Of The Breeze

Like a cowboy and his pony,
You ride and run all day,
With rattling spurs and bony
Limbs you gallop on your way.
You press your legs against the ground,
Wild *vaquero* of the breeze;
You swing your lasso round and round
To rope the hills and trees.

5. Pastoral

Like a herdsman with his cattle,
You give a cheerful call;
With smiling face, you rattle
On till you've corralled them all.
You are the pastor of the plains,
Tall companion of the breeze;
You are the maker of the rains
That changed our western destinies.

6. Siesta

But now *siesta* time has come;
Do not rattle, do not hum,
Do not swing your metal vanes,
Stately keeper of the plains.
Turn your petals from the sun,
For your daily work is done;
Like a sunflower in the sky
Bow your head when shadows fly.

"Like a herdsman with his cattle,
You give a cheerful call."

(Windmill, tanks, and cattle. Blue Mountains, Mason County. Photo by the author, 1976.)

THE WIND, THE WIND
THE TEXAS WIND

I am the wind, the blowing air;
I'm searching for you everywhere.
I turn your windmills, bring you rain,
And irrigate your fields of grain;
I keep you cool in summer days
When the sun descends in a fiery blaze;
In winter I bring you ice and snow
And give you an enchanted show;
But now I'm sorry I must complain.
The city dwellers caused me pain.
Deserted in my loneliness,
My desolation, I confess,
That suddenly the thought struck me
I'd also like to go to see
The city where the people stay.
And thus it happened, I regret to say,
That to their town I ventured forth;
There mighty buildings covered the earth.
They tortured me a hundredfold.
Though otherwise I am quite bold,
I barely escaped and away I flew
To woodland haunts, my rural view.
And now I know I'll not forget
How once I erred to my regret.
And still today I wince again
When I consider what happened then
As the city's misery I knew
And saw the metropolitan view.
And now I might as well confess:
The country is fair in its loneliness.
But some day I'll come back to town
And tear those mighty towers down.

"But some day I'll come back to town
And tear those mighty towers down."

(A storm over the skyline of a large Texas city. Photo, Texas Highway Department.)

"CROWN THINE ANCIENT CHURCH'S STORY"

All churches have a story they can tell;
Some are in Gothic style and have a bell.
A few are Romanesque with arches, round,
And there are those whose style makes not a sound.

Sometimes they will reflect their faith and creed;
Some show the world what they would preach and plead.
And we can crown the ancient church's story
With song and music that reveal its glory.

The Round Top church, beside a mighty tree,
Is sweet as any cedar chest can be.
The solid buttresses stand firm and strong
Against the buffeting of storms and wrong.

The Lindsay church is Romanesque, indeed,
Conservative, medieval, like its creed.
It rose again when a cyclone spread destruction;
The people went to work on new construction.

Saint Joseph's Church in down-town San Antone
Has character enough to stand like stone
And keep the large "Saint" Joske's store at bay.
Its German stations still lead you on today.

"The solid buttresses stand firm and strong
Against the buffeting of storms and wrong."

(Church at Round Top. The church is known for its inside cedar walls, its home-made organ, and the heavy buttresses. Photo by the author, 1970.)

Mission *Nuestra Señora Del Carmen* calls
Ysleta's Indians to come and seek its walls,
To worship in the chapel as of old
And get protection in the church's fold.

Westphalia has the largest wooden church;
Its double towers will aid you in your search
For restful, rural spots that lend you peace,
A pleasant respite, where all your troubles cease.

St. Olaf's *Kirke*, the "Rock Church" of today,
Once served Norwegian settlers on the way;
It still is host to weddings, as of old,
And festivals the people like to hold.

Saint Louis Church in Castroville still tells
Its message clearly and speaks with many bells;
The people worship in its Gothic hall,
While they can see its charm and hear its call.

Such is the church's story; it recalls
In many styles the message of it walls.
The steeples rise, the bells begin to ring,
While in the pews below the people sing.

"Westphalia has the largest wooden church;
Its double towers will aid you in your search."
(Church at Westphalia. Photo by the author, 1966.)

LOG BUILDINGS, U.S.A.

Log houses came to U.S.A. from Europe;
Became American like sorghum syrup.

Moravians, Swiss, and Swedes, and Germans, strong,
Brought axes, adzes, hammers, froes along.

They cut down trees and notched the logs together,
Then put in chinking to keep out hostile weather.

Soon Anglos added fireplaces, warm,
Built catted chimneys, with rustic, rural charm.

The roofs had gables that slept on logs and poles;
Then boards or shakes closed all the gaps and holes.

Log cabins came to Texas and joined the ranks
Of houses built of native stone and planks.

They stood beside adobe buildings there
That lent a Mexican fragrance to the air.

The German immigrants built *Fachwerk* places,
And left behind these homes with rugged faces.

Our aging houses beg for your protection;
Don't alter them; they do not need correction.

And now the age of logs has long since passed.
The age of trees? How long will all this last?

"Soon Anglos added fireplaces, warm,
Built catted chimneys, with rustic, rural charm."

(Walker County log cabin with catted chimney. Photo, courtesy, Terry G. Jordan, "Texas Log Cabin Register," North Texas State University.)

RURAL GOTHIC

The church's bell tolls far and wide:
"Come all, come all! With me abide!"
For many years the church has stood
And called her members as best she could:
    "Come, thou Fount of every blessing,
    Tune my heart to sing thy grace;
    Streams of mercy, never ceasing,
    Call for songs of loudest praise."
Inside, the seats in rigid rows
Are listening to the song and prayer,
Heavy benches through which flows
The music of the hymns, the air
Of singing voices, some deep, some thin,
All grateful for release from sin:
    "Amazing grace, how sweet the sound
    That saved a wretch like me!
    I once was lost, but now am found,
    Was blind, but now I see."
Long ago they all repented,
These pious people in the pews.
Each Sunday now they are contented
To hear anew the saving news:
    "There is a balm in Gilead,
    To make the wounded whole;
    There is a balm in Gilead,
    To heal the sin-sick soul."

"The church's bell tolls far and wide:
'Come all! Come all! With me abide.' "
(Methodist Church, Shelbyville. Photo by Jane Shivers Stroud, 1981.)

A pointed Gothic window tries
To lift its face again and rise,
But it is nailed upon the beam;
Its troubled forehead cannot dream;
It's crucified anew and dies:
    "There is a fountain filled with blood
    Drawn from Emanuel's veins;
    And sinners plunged beneath that flood
    Lose all their guilty stains."
The organ pipes its songs and wails
A saving tune that never fails;
It gives new hope for blessèd days
And sings a song of highest praise:
    "O for a thousand tongues to sing
    My great redeemer's praise.
    The glories of my God and King,
    The triumphs of his grace."
The preacher stands and reads the "Word,"
The well-known verses often heard,
Proclaiming his message to the crowd,
He raises his voice clear and loud.
And then the praying parson says:
"O God Almighty, come
And bless us in Thy home."

"For many years the church has stood
And called her members as best she could."
(Baptist Church, Waring. Photo by the author, 1981.)

THE LITTLE OLD SCHOOLHOUSE

By the country lane the little school stood;
Here children learned as best they could.
They opened their books, and the pages turned,
Then they recited what they had learned.

With forty pupils, more or less,
The teacher worked in great distress.
"Write the 'One-times-one' and the 'ABC'
Upon the board where all can see."

From McGruder's books they learned to read,
And blue-back spellers filled their need.
Then Texas hist'ry by Barker, *et al.*,
And Geography were taught to all.

"Sail on, O Ship of State," they said;
Then "The Psalm of Life" was often read,
And "Blessings on thee, little man,
Barfoot boy, with cheek of tan."

"Flow gently, sweet Afton," the singing began;
"My Bonnie lies over the Ocean," they sang.
Then came "My country, 'tis of thee;"
This was their land of liberty.

One game they played was "Red Rover, Red Rover."
They told their riddles over and over:
"First white as show, then green as clover,
Then red as blood, tastes good all over."

"With forty pupils, more or less,
The teacher worked in great distress."
(Mason County rural school, 1910. The teacher stands at the right.)

On Fridays the spelling matches were held,
And many words were pronounced and spelled,
Till one team spelled the other one down,
For which it received the victor's crown.

Then there was courting when springtime came;
You called the one you loved by name
And said: "You are my sweetheart, dear."
Your face turned red; someone might hear.

When the school year ended, there was a parade
From the little school to the creek bottom shade.
The children rode in wagons with streamers;
They sang and yelled — these happy screamers.

When the parade was over, the picnic came.
The pupils spoke verses of heroes and fame.
The "Concord Hymn" was often recited;
They all were stirred; they became excited.

The children presented a pantomime,
The old, old story of fleeting time:
"Backward, turn backward, o time in thy flight,
Make me a child again just for tonight."

And so it went from year to year.
Till time ran out, and the end was near.
The little school closed its windows and door,
Now all will forget, and none can restore.

"Write the 'One-times-one' and the 'A.B.C.'
Upon the board where all can see."

(Renner School Interior. The classroom was used until 1919. Now it is preserved in Old City Park, Dallas. Photo, by A. K. Barnett.)

THE OLD GARDENER

Old Max Meister had a gardener's hand,
All things he touched grew tall in the land.
And many a man knew deep in his heart
It was *Herr* Meister who gave him a start.
And while the breezes above him stirred,
The children and squirrels and birds all heard
How old Max Meister called to them all
When the ripened fruit began to fall:
"Come on over, little girl;
"Come on over, my son;
"I will give you something;
"I have a pecan."

When the autumn leaves were golden at dawn,
He stood beneath the towering pecan,
While the children passed by on their way to school.
Now old man Meister had made it a rule
To fill his pockets with the precious fruit
Whose kernels are sweet like the song of a flute.
He looked at the boys and the girls on the way
And thought, they'll be our leaders some day.
"Come on over, little girl;
"Come on over, my son;
"I will give you something;
"I have a pecan."

*"Old Max Meister had a gardener's hand,
All things he touched grew tall in the land."*
(Photo, The Austin-Travis County Collection, Austin Public Library.)

So the happy years rolled quietly by,
And old *Herr* Meister had to die.
Then young men carried him with their brawn
And buried him gently near his pecan.
While the voices of many, of matrons and men,
Began to sing and say "Amen,"
The children all gathered to say farewell
And mourn his going, for none could tell
    Who now would be waiting
    And calling at dawn:
    "Come on over, children;
    "I have a pecan."

But old Max Meister had made a plan:
The children should plant by his grave a pecan.
And many years after the day he died,
A thriving sapling arose by his side.
Now young and old declare they can hear
The voice of Max Meister calling near.
For every year when the nuts are falling,
Old *Herr* Meister's voice is calling:
    "Come on over, little girl;
    "Come on over, my son;
    "I will give you something;
    "I have a pecan."

"Come on over, little girl; Come on over my son;
I will give you something; I have a pecan."
(Photo, The Austin-Travis County Collection, Austin Public Library.)

THE WILD BUCK

Three hunters went out with visions of luck;
They went a-hunting to shoot the wild buck.

They lay down under a spreading oak;
They fell asleep, but their dreams awoke.

The first one:
I dreamed I beat upon the bush;
The buck sprang up and ran: swish, swush!

The second one:
And when the dogs pursued him and sprang,
I shot him with my gun: bing, bang!

The third one:
And when he fell to the ground, I saw
And blew my hunting horn: tra-rah!

Thus talked the three, but none would try,
When suddenly the buck ran by.

And ere the three hunters had seen him right,
He was gone over hill and dale in flight.
Swish, swush! Bing, bang! Tra-rah!

(Translated and adapted from Ludwig Uhland's
DER WEISSE HIRSCH, "The White Stag.")

"Three hunters went out with visions of luck;
They went a-hunting to shoot the wild buck."

(A white-tailed deer buck in the Texas Hill Country. Photo, R. B. Pumphrey Collection, Eugene C. Barker Texas History Center, The University of Texas.)

THE BOVINES' FATE

On lonely ranches they lie or stand
And breathe the trembling sky.
The sun weights heavy on the land;
They know not how nor why.

In all the summer solitude
They soon forget the blast
Of icy storms that did intrude
Into their rural past.

They do not know their end is near,
And slaughter houses wait.
The open hills are always here,
And they must meet their fate.

"They do not know their end is near,
And slaughter houses wait."

(Cattle by an earthen water tank in the Texas Hill Country. Photo, Kilman Studio, Fredericksburg, Texas.)

BLACK BLOOD

Black blood is flowing in the ground;
We thrust in needles where veins are found.
The pulse is throbbing, the pressure, strong;
The drills are humming their earthy song.
We fill our tanks, supply our needs,
While Mother Earth lies still and bleeds.

"We fill our tanks, supply our needs,
While Mother Earth lies still and bleeds."

(Boom-time oil derrick in Gregg County, 1930. Photo, East Texas Oil Museum, Kilgore.)

SONG OF THE CLOUD

I dream in sleepy skies
Where fabled castles rise;
A song at noon,
And very soon
I build your mansions of romance,
And at a glance
I mold your fancy's bold desires:
Domes or spires.
I spin the legends, wise,
Where lore, abundant, lies.
I place a beam
Of beauty in your dream;
I take a glow
Of color and a gleam
Of joy and bliss
By which I know
Love's synthesis,
For I live in the southern sky
Where love and romance lie.

"I mold your fancy's bold desires:
Domes or spires."
(Clouds in East Texas. Photo by the author, 1968.)

COUNTY COURTHOUSES

Courthouses like to live on central squares;
On every side, invite the people's stares.
But others stand aside, as houses do;
They show their faces boldly and greet you too.

Some county capitols have central towers;
These ancient symbols now portray new powers.
Then there are domes, their turtle heads withdrawn;
They have to stretch their necks to greet the dawn.

The buildings often boast a booming clock
That strikes so hard it almost cracks a rock.
And all the people set their clocks and watches,
So that the boomer every time piece matches.

Some county houses have a funny style;
If you don't laugh, you'll surely want to smile.
For often there's a puzzling, awkward stance,
So nondescript, as if it grew by chance.

But these old houses help to stabilize
Your life, this peaceful world you visualize,
Because the law brings justice, and you can be
Assured of happiness and liberty.

And all in all, there is not better place
To meet and greet the mighty public's face.
You talk your piece and make political plots
And hope that they will leave no ugly spots.

"And all in all, there is no better place
To meet and greet the mighty public's face."
(Courthouse, Denton County. Photo by the author, 1981.)

TEXAS CAPITOL

This is a shrine that all may come to see
And consecrate a life of liberty.
A goddess crowns the lofty capitol dome
And towers above the people's civic home.

You can come in and celebrate the past
To unify anew this state, so vast;
And then review terrazzo floor designs,
The battles won that history refines.

In glorious colors, the words of "Alamo,"
Of "San Jacinto" and others shine and glow.
Beneath the dome the nations' seals are shown,
Whose flags above the lone star state have flown.

You may come in and watch the statesmen stare
At you from walls, that could, of course, be bare.
They pose for you in dignity above;
They're always there and never dare to move.

Its walls of granite are steady, calm, and strong,
Like an enchanted rock; yet like a song
Its graceful lines lend it a gentle air,
Inviting like the western skies, so fair.

"This is a shrine that all may come to see
And consecrate a life of liberty."
(Texas State Capitol. Photo by the author, 1979.)

ELISABET NEY

In Germany she carved the kings, the great,
Philosophers and rulers, and her mate:
King Ludwig, Bismark, Humboldt, Schopenhauer.
She carved and shaped and lent them lasting power.
She was ambitious, talented, and fair;
To be the greatest sculptress she would dare.
Montgomery, her doctor husband, too,
Had lofty goals of what some day he'd do.
All through their lives, few people ever knew
How great her talent, and how profound his view.
The Texas air brought inspiration, true:
She carved Sam Houston and made his stature new;
And Stephen Austin through her achievement grew.
They stand like sentinels at the state house portals
To greet the folk as heroes and as mortals.

"She carved Sam Houston and made his stature new;
And Stephen Austin through her achievement grew."

(Elizabet Ney at work in her studio. Photo, courtesy, Eugene C. Barker Texas History Center, The University of Texas.)

FLOWER FACES

Who could be sad when nature is so fair,
And fragrance of the flowers fills the air?
The birds have more to say when flowers they see,
And butterflies flit aimlessly 'round me.

We sip from WINE CUPS, red as Burgundy.
The DAISY turns her face the sun to see.
We watch the COREOPSIS sway and nod,
While SENSITIVE BRIAR sleeps calmly on the sod.

A TEXAS STAR is blushing pink and coy,
The BLACK-EYED SUSANS' waving brings us joy;
And lavender VERBENAS hope and wait
That we might come and see their happy state.

By lichen-covered, weathered granite rocks,
Peer forth, bright-eyed, the pink and reddish PHLOX.
Nearby, BLUEBONNETS and scarlet PAINTBRUSH stand,
Alert and straight, and wait to shake your hand.

INDIAN BLANKETS love the Texas prairies,
And DANDELIONS turn to fluffy fairies.
THISTLES blow amid their prickly spines;
Whoever plucks them off soon weeps or whines.

PRIMROSES, BUTTERCUPS and POPPIES plead:
"Leave us alone, so we can grow our seed."
The DOGWOOD and the REDBUD trees proclaim:
"Don't cut our limbs; we'll never be the same."

CACTUS plants are blooming yellow and red,
But everywhere their vicious thorns are spread.
Like rattlesnakes, they wait to use their fangs;
As victim you will suffer pain and pangs.

Such is the atmosphere of Texas Wild
That you may come attired as nature's child.
You surely will be happy as a guest
Of all the Texas flowers at their best.

*"Nearby, BLUEBONNETS and scarlet PAINTBRUSH stand,
Alert and straight, and wait to shake your hand."*

(Close-up view of bluebonnets, the Texas state flower. Photo, Courtesy, *Texas Highways*."

TEXAS, THE FESTIVAL STATE

Cinco de Mayo is a Mexican freedomfest;
The people dance *fandangos* and do their best
To celebrate *fiestas* all day long
With *enchiladas, tacos,* and with song.

New Braunfels has a *Wurstfest* every year,
Where *Opas* serve up barrels of *Lagerbier*;
The oompah bands blare out their songs, well chosen,
And *Dirndl* dresses twirl 'round *Lederhosen.*

To Huntsville comes Sam Houston on his day;
Then many ladies dress in costumes gay.
And by his side stands pretty Margaret Lea;
That she's no Indian, everyone can see.

The Llano Valley German Methodists hold
A Hymnfest, where they sing as once of old;
They sing: "I know a river's glorious stream,"
And add: "It shines and glows in a fiery gleam."

In Fredericksburg the Easter fires glow,
And in the nearby hills wild flowers grow.
The children pluck them off and take them home
To build their nests for *Osterhas'* to come.

The Folklife Festival in San Antone
Displays the various people and what they've done.
The Institute of Texan Cultures shows
The various ethnic groups, their joys and woes.

"Cinco de Mayo is a Mexican freedomfest:
The people dance fandangos and do their best. . . ."
(Mexican dancers in La Villita, San Antonio. Photo, *Texas Highways.*)

In Palo Duro the *Texas* pageant plays,
Depicting there the life of former days;
Against the cliff, the brilliant lightning flashes,
And all around the mighty thunder crashes.

Saint Louis' Celebration in Koenig Park
Is Castroville's one-hundred-year-old work;
Across the town the people worship first
And then they dance and eat and quench their thirst.

In Van Zandt County (Or is it perhaps a state?)
"First Monday" is a time to celebrate,
And people come to Canton town to trade
A horse and buggy, a casserole, or spade.

To powwows and fish-frys everybody goes,
To cookoffs, walkfests, jubilees, and shows.
There are the Juneteenth Freedomfests for Blacks,
Songfests for Germans, and *Sokol Flets* for Czechs.

From East and West, from North and South they run
A thousand miles or so to have their fun;
These Texans come to see it all and learn it,
From Paint Rock, Shiner, Tenaha, and Burnet.

"New Braunfels has a Wurstfest every year,
Where Opas serve up barrels of Lagerbier."
(Photo, courtesy, *Texas Highways.*)

VARIATIONS ON THE THEME OF THE YELLOW ROSE

The Yellow Rose of Texas wore
Her pretty tresses long,
Bewitched her lover, and he swore
His love to her in song:
"Forget the Belles of Tennessee
And leave your Nellie Bly,
The Yellow Rose is my destiny,
For her I'll ever sigh.

"I left her, and she cried for me,
And tears as bright as dew
Flowed down her cheeks, and I could see
Her love was ever new.
Our parting gave us hurt and pain,
But then the sky turned blue;
And when some day we meet again,
We'll be forever true."

"And when some day we meet again,
We'll be forever true."

(Cover of the David W. Guion version of "The Yellow Rose of Texas," 1936. Photo by Jeanne Deis Studio, Dallas. Printed with permission of G. Shirmer, Inc.

PLAY PARTY SONG

Pepper grows
On a pepper tree,
Water flows
To the deep, blue sea.

My love is true,
As true can be;
Whate'er she'll do
Is done for me.

Go in and out
The window here
And trip about
Without a fear.

Now let us sing
Our little song.
We'll dance a fling
And skip along.

"Now let us sing our little song.
We'll dance a fling and skip along."
(A folk dance scene. Photo, Texas Highway Department.)

MEDLEY OF OLD FOLK SONGS

Bring in the fiddle and make it sing,
Play the guitar and let it ring,
Stand up together, let's sing an air:
Johnny crack corn, and I don't care.

Ol' Dan Tucker had an iron beard,
But he was a man no one ever feared;
He played the banjo an' the fife,
And swung the ladies all his life.

I am a Texas cowboy and ride the Texas range;
Get along, little dogies; you'll travel for a change.
If I get back to Texas, I nevermore will roam,
For I'm a Texas cowboy, far away from home.

Lost my partner; what'll I do?
Go to the party and skip to my Lou;
Cows in the cornfield; what'll I do?
Go to the party and skip to my Lou.

If I can't find and dance with Josie,
I'll take to Susan Brown or Rosie.
Black-eyed Susie is a sunburnt daisy;
If I can't get her, I'll go crazy.

"Bring in the fiddle and make it sing,
Play the guitar and let it ring."
(Participant in an old fiddlers' reunion. Photo, courtesy, *Texas Highways*.)

Frankie shot her man; he done her wrong;
And now we hear about them in a song.
No way to help them, no way to save,
And Johnny lies a-mould'rin' in the grave.

When you and I were young, Maggie,
We rode together in a courting buggy.
She held her parasol and smiled;
In the lonesome valley we were beguiled.

Then to the little church we all will go
And we will sing the spirituals high and low.
Maggie reads the notes, and her lover hums:
"We'll all sing Hallelujah when He comes."

"When you and I were young, Maggie,
We rode together in a courting buggy."
(The author and his child bride, 1926)

TWO GOVERNORS FOR THE PRICE OF ONE

Farmer Jim Ferguson was twice elected
And served until he was ejected,
Impeached from office and the governor's chair;
But Fergusonism was in the air.

Eight years later, Ma took his place,
When the "vest-pocket" vote won the governor's race.
"Two for the price of one," Pa said,
And Miriam Ferguson was the state's new head.

Pa was *de facto* governor
Until Ma Ferguson's terms were o'er.
"Bread Bonds" were issued, the needy were fed,
And convicts were freed while the Fergusons led.

" 'Pa was de facto governor
Until 'Ma' Ferguson's terms were o'er."

(Governors Jim and Mariam Ferguson casting "vest pocket votes." Photo, 1944, in the Eugene C. Barker Texas History Center, The University of Texas.)

PAISANO OF THE BRUSH COUNTRY

Frank Dobie knew the brush like a *paisano*;
His trusted friends were Anglo and *Chicano*.
The droughts depressed him when he was still a lad;
Dry trees and thirsty cattle made him sad.

He loved the ranches well, but went away
To seek his future in academia's way.
This brought the world of books and romance too,
And Bertha soon became his love, so true.

And as the Brownings wrote each other rhymes,
So Frank and Bertha wrote a hundred times;
Prose, to be sure, but winsome lines *per se*,
Their letters treat of love and her strange way.

Yet fabled longhorns, mustangs, and coyotes
Stayed with him always and turned to words and notes.
And he corralled tall tales while in his saddle
As cowboys hunt and round up straying cattle.

He felt at home on marble floors or grass,
And he could ride old Buck right into class.
He wore his boots and walked with English dons
Across the manicured, collegiate lawns.

"And he corralled tall tales while in his saddle
As cowboys hunt and round up straying cattle."

(J. Frank Dobie, 1888-1964, professor, folklorist, and author at the University of Texas. Photo in the Dobie Collection, Humanities Research Center. The University of Texas.)

Frank was irascible like cat claw brush;
To keep at peace with him, you had to hush.
Unorthodox and curious like coyotes,
He championed rebel causes, but lacked the votes.

No friend of research and of Ph.D.'s;
These things were cold to him as winter's freeze.
Cowpeople's talk, he said, had more to offer,
And professorial lectures made him suffer.

Life on the range was dear to Dobie's heart,
But flowers and thorns grew never far apart,
And he belonged to the bitter lovely land;
This was his world, and here he took his stand.

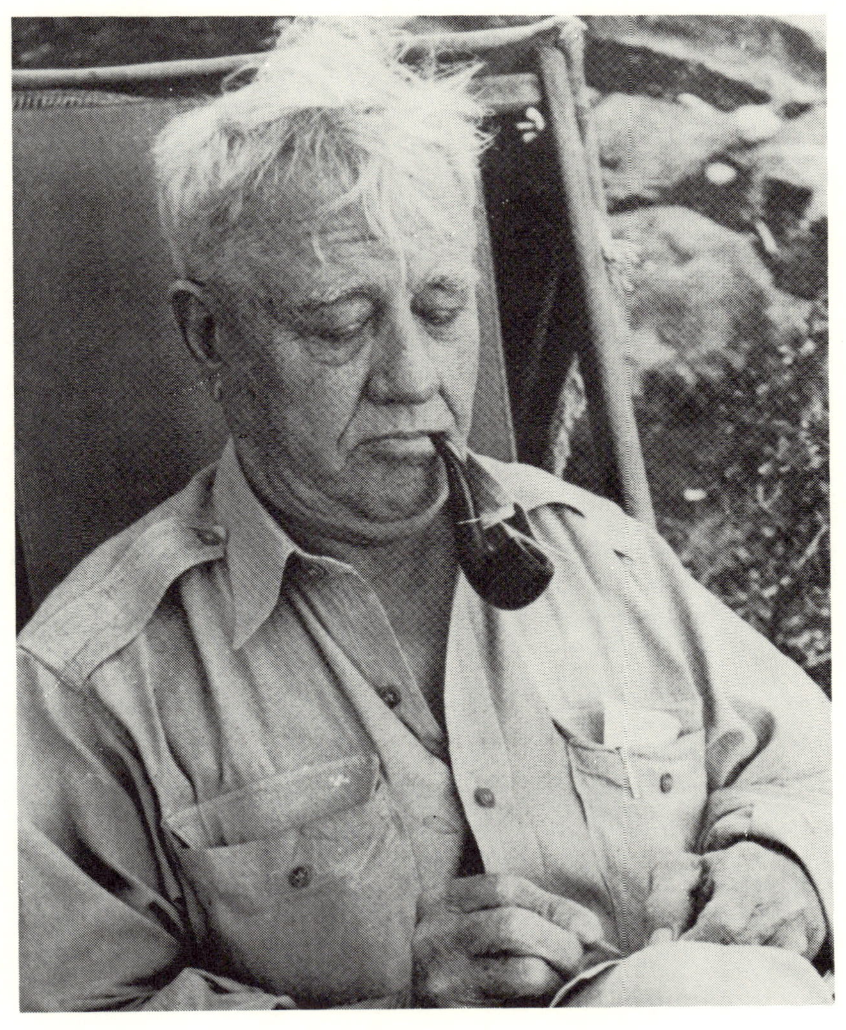

"No friend of research and of Ph.D.'s;
These things were cold to him as winter's freeze."

(J. Frank Dobie, 1888-1964. Photo in the Eugene C. Barker Texas History Center, The University of Texas.)

PRINCE OF PEDERNALES

Lyndon Johnson was of cowboy size,
So were his ears, but not his searching eyes.
He looked right through a man and he could see
If this might be a friend or enemy.

He went to college, but such was not his dish,
And politics became his greatest wish.
The Prince of Pedernales he might be;
In Stetson hats he felt at ease and free.

He could be ruthless if he felt the need,
And he would never let himself be treed;
But he was also friendly in his ways,
If he could read compassion in your gaze.

Lyndon moved as Texas northers blow,
His speed and pace knew only high, no low;
And like the land from which he issued forth,
He was both harsh and gentle; this was his earth.

He drove his Lincoln Continental fast,
And liked it much; it was his size and cast.
He steered his floating car into the river
To make the frightened riders quake and quiver.

He had his way with folk and could be nice;
His smile could also be as cold as ice.
As president, he did not push, indeed,
He took you by your coat lapels to lead.

"The Prince of Pedernales he might be;
In Stetson hats he felt at ease and free."
(Lyndon Baines Johnson, 1909-1973, 36th President of the U.S.A., 1963-69. Photo, courtesy, L.B.J. Library, Austin.)

He met Miss Taylor — they called her Lady Bird —
And now her real name is seldom heard.
Bird knew that she had roped a Texas steer,
But as a country girl she had no fear.

When JFK and LBJ joined hands,
They won the votes in many states and lands;
They sat and spoke in salty words together,
And what they talked about was not the weather.

He was not born to make the old be new,
Yet left behind reforms, both great and true.
And Lady Bird would beautify the land;
She had an eye for beauty and a gardener's hand.

He loved the land and worked for preservation.
Our prized resources needed conservation.
For this his ranch serves as a model place;
Here you can see our country's smiling face.

"For this his ranch serves as a model place;
Here you can see our country's smiling face."

(L.B.J. ranch house and grazing cattle by the Pedernales River. Photo, courtesy, The L.B.J. Library, Austin.)

LON TINKLE, COSMOPOLITE

Lon was as French as Balzac and Racine,
His mind alert, his thoughts were free and keen.
He was sophisticated and refined,
The Duke of Windsor and Montesquieu combined.
He was all French, and no Germanophile,
But Goethe's greatness he could accept and feel.
A Texan, too, like DeGolyer and Frank Dobie.
How could this be? — He never drove a dogie.
He wrote of Texas and the Alamo,
Its brave defense and then the final blow;
Yet he himself was gentle as a dove.
No man of war was he; he stood above
The harsh realities of strife and war
And saw the fights and battles from afar.
His wife Maria was hispanic as a *fiesta*;
He won her heart in one grand, bold *conquista*.

"He was sophisticated and refined,
The Duke of Windsor and Montesquieu combined."

(Lon Tinkle, Southern Methodist University professor for many years. Staff photo. Courtesy, S.M.U. Public Relations Department.)

WALTER PRESCOTT WEBB, INC.

Walter Prescott Webb incorporated
A company of friends, quite dedicated;
They all agreed, no matter what his views,
And what he wrote they took for fact or news.

Webb was a man with influence far and near,
A scholar, tough as any Texas steer,
More as a thinker who reasoned out the facts,
Than as a chronicler of deeds and acts.

His interest in *belles lettres* and folklore too
Shows what a friend like Dobie does for you.
He knew how earthbound deeds and facts can be,
Whereas in literature we soar and see.

He showed us how the Colt revolver shoots,
And how the West was won with guns and boots.
He swept across *The Great Frontier* and saw
How man moved westward as though by natural law.

He stood for right, if need be, all alone,
A man in whom the light of freedom shone;
He climbed from harsh adversity to fame,
Yet never could forget from where he came.

When Webb died in an auto accident,
There were no pioneers; his life was spent.
What tragedy that such a man should fall
In modern traffic, far from the frontier's call.

"Webb was a man with influence far and near,
A scholar, tough as any Texas steer."

(Walter Prescott Webb, 1888-1963, professor and author at the University of Texas for many years. Photo, presented by Mrs. Webb to the Eugene C. Barker Texas History Center, The University of Texas.)

"Campmeetings, too, and rural Gothic singing
Are past; and church bells soon will cease their ringing."

(Group of campers at Mason County campmeeting. Brush arbor and tents in the background. Photo, courtesy, Mrs. Sam Eckert.)

AFTERWORD

They all are gone: Chief Quanah's hunting realm,
The *Padres*, Houston, Johnson lost their helm.

The Alamo no longer guards her men;
The buffaloes will not stampede again.

The Yellow Rose has lost her youthful charm,
And old man Cooter no longer brings alarm.

Elisabet Ney and Cynthia Ann now lie
In burial plots, and cowboys say "Goodbye."

The ancient church and Mission San José,
Great River, all are now so far away.

Walt Webb and windmills, all are fading fast;
Lon Tinkle's time and Dobie's days are past.

Ma Ferguson and pioneer woman knew
How fast their days of prime passed out of view.

Log buildings now have gained nostalgic favor;
But who still lives in them and likes their flavor?

Campmeetings, too, and rural Gothic singing
Are past; and church bells soon will cease their ringing.

Herr Meister and his children all are gone;
He can't come back and hand out a pecan.

The little school beside the country lane
No longer calls; its walls begin to wane.

Play parties and the songs of Susan Brown
Have gone away from our little town.

But rains will fall and rivers seaward flow,
While flowers of the hills put on their show.

Folksongs and festivals forever stay,
And we will sing, while happy children play.

"But rains will fall and rivers seaward flow,
While flowers of the hills put on their show."
(Black-eyed Susans in Mason County. Photo by the author, 1975.)

BIBLIOGRAPHY AND SUGGESTED READINGS

Abernethy, Francis Edward, editor, *Legendary Ladies of Texas*. (Publications of the Texas Folklore Society, Number 53). Dallas: E. Heart Press, 1981.

Abernethy, Francis Edward, editor. *The Folklore of Texan Cultures*. (Publications of the Texas Folklore Society, Number 38). Austin: The Encino Press, 1974.

Ajilvsgi, Geyata, *Wild Flowers of the Big Thicket, East Texas, and Western Louisiana*. College Station and London: Texas A&M University Press, 1979.

Baker, T. Lindsay, *The First Polish Americans*. College Station and London: Texas A&M University Press, 1979.

Biesele, Rudolph Leopold, *The History of the German Settlements in Texas, 1831-1861*. Austin: Press of Von Boeckmann-Jones Co., 1930.

Driskill, Frank A. and Noel Grisham, *Historic Churches of Texas*. Austin: Eakin Press, 1980.

Fehrenbach, T. R., *Lone Star: A History of Texas and Texans*. New York: MacMillan Publishing Co., Inc., 1968.

Friend, Llerna B., *Sam Houston: The Great Designer*. Austin and London: University of Texas Press, 1954.

Gambrell, Herbert and Virginia, *A Pictorial History of Texas*. New York: E. P. Dutton & Co., Inc., 1960.

Habig, Fr. Marion A., O.F.M., *San Antonio's Mission San José*. The Naylor Co., 1968.

Horgan, Paul, *Great River: The Rio Grande in North American History*. New York and Toronto: Rinehart & Company, 1954.

James, Marquis, *The Raven: A Biography of Sam Houston*. New York: Blue Ribbon Books, Inc., 1929.

Jordan, Gilbert J., *The Morning Is Not Far: Some Poems*. Dallas: Published by the author, 1974.

Jordan, Gilbert J., *Yesterday in the Texas Hill Country*. College Station and London: Texas A&M University Press, 1979.

Jordan, Terry G., "Population Origin Groups in Rural Texas," Map Supplement, Number 13, *Annals of the Association of American Geographers*, Vol. 60, No. 2, June, 1970.

Jordan, Terry G., *Texas Log Buildings: A Folk Architecture*. Austin and London: University of Texas Press, 1978.

King, Irene Marschall, *John O. Meusebach: German Colonizer in Texas*. Austin & London: University of Texas Press, 1967.

Lich, Glen E., *The German Texans*. San Antonio: The University of Texas Institute of Texan Cultures, 1981.

Lomax, John A. and Alan Lomax, *Best Loved American Folk Songs*. New York: Grosset & Dunlap, 1947.

McGuire, Jack, and Mac Tatchell, *A President's Country: A Guide to the LBJ Country of Texas*. Austin: Shoal Creek Publishers, Inc., 1965, 1973.

Methodist Hymnal. Edited by the Hymnal Committee, Edwin E. Voigt, Chairman. Nashville: The Methodist Publishing House, 1966.

Olmsted, Frederick Law, *A Journey Through Texas: Or a Saddle-Trip On the Southwestern Frontier*, with a Foreword by Larry McMurtry. New Reprint. Austin & London: University of Texas Press, 1978.

Owens, William A., *Tell Me a Story, Sing Me a Song*. Austin: University of Texas Press, 1983.

Owens, William A., *Three Friends: Roy Bedichek, J. Frank Dobie, Walter Prescott Webb*. Austin and London: University of Texas Press, 1967 & 1975.

Ramsdell, Charles, *San Antonio: A Historical and Pictorial Guide*. Austin & London: University of Texas Press, 1968.

Smith, Erwin E. (photos) and J. Evetts Haley (text), *Life on the Texas Range*. Austin: University of Texas Press, 1952.

Stephens, I. K., *The Hermit Philosopher of Liendo*. Dallas: Southern Methodist University Press, 1951. (This book deals with Dr. Edmund Montgomery and Elisabet Ney).

Texas Legislative Council, *The Texas Capitol: Building a Capitol and a Great State*. Austin: Texas Highway Department, 1975.

Tinkle, Lon, *An American Original: The Life of J. Frank Dobie*. Boston & Toronto: Little, Brown and Company, 1978.

Tinkle, Lon, *The Alamo*. New York: New American Library (Signet Books), 1958. Original title: *13 Days to Glory*. New York: McGraw-Hill, 1958.

Turner, Martha Anne, *The Yellow Rose of Texas: The Story of a Song*. El Paso: Texas Western Press, The University of Texas at El Paso, 1973.

Webb, Walter Prescott, *The Great Frontier*. Austin: University of Texas Press, 1951 . . . 1975.

Wills, Mary Matz, and Howard S. Irwin, *Roadside Flowers of Texas*. Austin: University of Texas Press, 1969.

INDEX OF WORDS AND NAMES

Alcalde, Spanish word for *judge*.

Amerinds, American Indians.

Baroque is a style of architecture noted for ornate decorations and statues.

Belles lettres, French for *beautiful letters*, literature as one of the fine arts.

Bertha McKee, wife of J. Frank Dobie.

"Black blood," petroleum.

"Blue Norther" is a sudden and frigid Texas north wind. One of several words used to describe the windmills in the poems under this title.

Bly, Nellie. The name occurs in the German version of "The Yellow Rose of Texas." (see Yellow Rose.)

Brazos de Dios, Spanish for *Arms of God*, the Brazos River.

Browning, Robert and Elizabeth Barrett, famous 19th century English poets.

Buck. — J. Frank Dobie's favorite horse.

Cajuns is a Louisiana-French word derived from *Acadians*. These French-speaking people were expelled from Acadia in Nova Scotia by the British, and they settled in New Iberia, Louisiana. See Longfellow's *Evangeline*.

Catted chimneys are made of mud plastered over poles, sticks, and pliable strips, called "cats."

Chalk Mountain is a small community in Erath County on Hwy. 67, between Glen Rose and Stephenville. The unusual Swiss barn referred to in the poem "Pioneers All" was described and its heritage traced to Swiss prototypes by Terry G. Jordan in "A Forebay Bank Barn in Texas," *Pennsylvania Folklife*, Winter, 1980-81, Vol. 30, No. 2, 72-77.

Cherokee, one of the five civilized Indian tribes. Sam Houston lived for some time among the Cherokees before he came to live in Texas.

Chicanos, hispanics. Many younger Mexican-Americans and the more recent immigrants prefer the word *Chicano* over other designations, such as *Latin-Americans* or *Mexican-Americans*.

Cinco de Mayo, Spanish for May 5, Mexican Independence Day.

The "Coffeemill" building in Fredericksburg is called the *Kaffeemühle* in German. It was the *Vereinskirche*, the Immigration Society's church or community building. It was built in 1847, razed in 1897, and rebuilt in 1935.

"Come thou Fount of every blessing" and other hymns quoted in the poem "Rural Gothic" are familiar songs.

Conquista, Spanish for *conquest*.

Cooter, a fictitious name.

Coushatta. The Alabama-Coushatta Indians have maintained their Piney-Woods Reservation between Livingston and Woodville in Polk Co., on Hwy. 190.

The Czechs established several colonies in Texas. See the Terry Jordan map.

Dirndl, German for *young girl. Dirndl* dresses, German-Bavarian costumes.

Dogie, Western dialect word for a stray or motherless calf.

Eighteen forty-five is the year in which many German Colonists came to Texas under the auspices of the "Society for the Protection of German Immigrants in Texas." Many of them died at the port of Indianola and in New Braunfels and Fredericksburg.

Easter nests. In the German settlements of Texas the children picked wild flowers and built nests for the Easter rabbit (*Osterhas'*) to put in the eggs.

Enchiladas, tacos, typical Texas-Mexican foods.

El Sol Colorado, Spanish for *The Red Sun*, a name applied by the Indians to red-beard John O. Meusebach.

Fachwerk, German for *half-timbered* house construction.

Fandango, a Mexican dance.

Feste, German for *festivals*.

Fiestas, Spanish for *festivals*.

Froe, a tool used to prepare boards, etc. for log buildings.

Goethe, famous German poet.

Gothic, a medieval style of architecture, characterized by large, pointed, stained-glass windows.

Herr, German for *Mister, Lord.*

Houston, Sam (1793-1863) was a strong opponent of secession and was deposed from the governorship when he refused to swear allegiance to the Confederacy. The story of his conversion and his baptism in Rocky Creek in 1854 appears in Marquis James' book *The Raven*, p. 385.

Indian corn, ordinary corn.

Indianola, a former city on Matagorda Bay, the main port of entry of the German immigrants in the mid-nineteenth century. It was destroyed later by a hurricane.

"Jimmy Crack Corn," a folk song.

Josie, Susan Brown, Frankie, Johnny, and Maggie are all names occurring in folk songs.

Chief Katemoczy was one of several Indian leaders taking part in the Meusebach Indian Treaty on the San Saba River in 1847. The little village of Katemcy in Mason County was named for Katemoczy.

Kirke, Norwegion for *church.*

Lagerbier, German beer.

Lederhosen, German leather shorts used in Bavarian folk costumes.

MacKenzie, Col. Ranald, was one of the best Indian fighters in Texas in the 1870s. It was he and his men who struck the final blow against Quanah Parker and the Indians at Palo Duro in 1874. See T. R. Fehrenbach's *Lone Star*, 542-551.

Matagorda Bay is on the Gulf of Mexico between Galveston and Corpus Christi. Here many of the German immigrants landed in the 1840s in boats arriving from Galvestion, where sailing ships had brought them from Bremen and Antwerp. Because of lack of facilities at Indianola, hundreds of people perished here.

Meister, Max, is a fictitious name.

Meusebach, John O., German colonizer, founder of Fredericksburg, and initiator of the treaty with the Indians.

Mission San José (St. Joseph), built in 1720, is perhaps the best of the Spanish missions at San Antonio. It has been partially restored, not only the main church, but also the Indian huts, the granary, and the mill.

Montgomery, Dr. Edmund, English physician and philosopher, husband of Elisabet Ney. The couple came to the U.S.A. in 1871 and to Texas in 1873.

Nederland is a Dutch settlement between Beaumont and Port Arthur.

Ney, Elisabet, famous German sculptress, settled near Hempstead and later in Austin. Among her well known American pieces are the statues of Stephen F. Austin and Sam Houston, now standing in the capitol of Texas.

Nuestra Señora del Carmen, Spanish for *Our Lady of Carmen*, the name of the Ysleta Mission near El Paso.

Opas, German for *Grandpas*. At the New Braunfels *Wurstfest* (Sausage Festival), the waiters or hosts are called *Opas* (Grandpas).

Osterhas', German for *Easter rabbit.*

"The Bovines' Fate" was suggested by a drawing by Thomas W. Shefelman of Austin.

Padre, Spanish for *Father, Priest.*

Panna Maria, the Polish mother colony in Texas, near San Antonio.

Paisano, Spanish word for *road runner, chaparral bird.* The original and basic meaning is *fellow countryman.*

Parker, Cynthia Ann, was kidnapped by the Indians at Parker's Fort in 1836 and adopted by the Indians. Peta Nocona took her as his mate. Her son Quanah led the Indians in various battles in the 1870s, such as Palo Duro and Adobe Walls. He ended up on the Indian Territories in Oklahoma.

Pastoral, from *pastor, shepherd*, or *herdsman*, later also applied to *clergyman.* One of the several words used to describe the windmills in the poem by this name.

Per se, Latin for *inherently.*

Play party, a social gathering of young people. At these home parties, games of parading, rythmic skipping around, swinging of hands, etc., accompanied by folk songs were played. The play party was similar to the square dance.

Prairie schooner is a large covered wagon used by American pioneers in crossing the western plains. One of several words used to describe windmills in the poems by this title.

The Raven, the name the Indians gave to Sam Houston.

Romanesque, medieval style of architecture.

"Rural Gothic" is the title of a painting by Grant Wood.

St. Joske's. The Joske's Store in San Antonio is facetiously called St. Joske's because it almost surrounds St. Joseph's Church.

Santa Anna, Mexican general and president during the Texas War of Independence.

Siesta, Spanish word for *a brief nap*. It means literally the *sixth hour*. This is one of several words used to describe windmills in the poems under this title.

"Skip to my Lou," is a play-party folk song.

Taylor, Claudia, wife of President Johnson (Lady Bird Johnson).

Terrazzo, flooring made of small chips of colored marble, set in cement and polished. Some of the best terrazzo in Texas is to be found in the State Capitol.

"Texas Cowboy" is a folk song.

Texicans, alternate form of the word *Texans*, used in the 19th century.

Tinkle, Lon, author of books on the Alamo, Degolyer, Frank Dobie, etc., professor at Southern Methodist University, famous book reviewer, critic, and connoisseur.

Tucker, Dan, is a folk-song character.

Uhland, Ludwig, early 19th century German poet.

Vaquero, Spanish for *cowboy*, one of several words used to describe windmills in the poems under this title.

"The White Stag" (*Der weisse Hirsch*) is a familiar German poem by Ludwig Uhland. The main adaptation in the present author's English version is the substitution of *oak* for *Tannenbaum* (fir tree) and *wild buck* for *der weisse Hirsch* (*the white stag*).

The Wends were Slavic people from the Spree River near Berlin, Germany. They were bilingual, Wendish and German. Their mother colony was Serbin, near Giddings. Here they built a beautiful rural Lutheran church.

Wurstfest, German for *Sausage Festival* held every year in New Braunfels.

Yellow Rose. "The Yellow Rose of Texas" is a familiar folk song composed anonymously after the Battle of San Jacinto. For further details see the Martha Anne Turner book. — The words *Nellie Bly* occur in the German version of the song, 1906, quoted by Turner, pp. 14-15.